Knifery

Complete Handbook

of

Knife

Care & Safety

Robert Clemente

Knifery

Complete Handbook
of
Knife
Care & Safety
...with Camping & Outdoor Tips

by

Robert Clemente

1st Edition, 2nd Printing

Knifery, Complete Handbook of Knife Care and Safety
ISBN 9781077701861
Copyright 2006/2019 by Robert Clemente
Major Market Publications
Newnan GA 30265

Manuscript writing, illustrations, compilation, and production
by Robert Clemente, Atlanta, Georgia
Pagination and preparation
by Caroline Fike, Greenville, Tennessee
Manuscript consultant content edit proof
by David Swinden, Schrade Cutlelry, Ellenville, New York

Contents

Dedications

This book is dedicated to the generations of knife makers who made Schrade knives. Imperial Schrade Corp., Schrade Cutlery, closed its doors in the summer of 2004, after 100 years of excellent knife and tool making. Their craftsmanship is legendary, and the products of the highest quality. To own just one Schrade knife is to have a part of history itself in your pocket. The people who made the Schrade knives and tools would hope that you enjoy your knife and tool products and that this book will help you with knife knowledge, care, and handling safety. Whether you are a casual collector, consumer, or serious knife aficionado, this book will help you in your appreciation and passion for the knife and its purposes.

And a personal remembrance, to Robert Greene (1931-2016), my "church dad" and outdoor enthusiast and mentor whose love, outdoor guidance, and personal leadership... without which, this book could not have been conceived and written.

Introduction

A knife from an established manufacturer is a well designed and quality built product that will serve you for many years if you use it properly and take care of it. There is a certain sense of pride in owning a knife, and with that ownership comes responsibility, to yourself and to others. Your knife is a tool to help you, and to do work for you. Do not see it as a toy or a weapon to hurt others. Like any other tool, you must take care of it so when you need a job done, the knife will be ready to work for you.

There are many things that a knife can do, and many things a knife cannot do. Understanding how to properly use, take care of, and store your knife will help you to appreciate its design, function, and use. Whether you are on a short camping trip, working in the backyard, or on a survival hike, knowing how to properly use your knife will help you get the most from it.

Knife Knowledge

A knife is not just a sharp piece of metal with a handle. It is a precision tool designed to do a host of tasks. Knives are designed with specific purposes in mind. Get to know your knife and what its purpose is. The blade design, the handle, how it opens and closes, the blade material, all are a part of its design and intended function.

The basic shape of the blade is the first clue as to its cutting purpose. The length, thickness, shape, cutting edge, and blade size, all have a part in the function the designers and cutlers had in mind when they built the knife. Certain blades have very specific purposes while others are built for general use.

Pocket Knife Blade Shapes

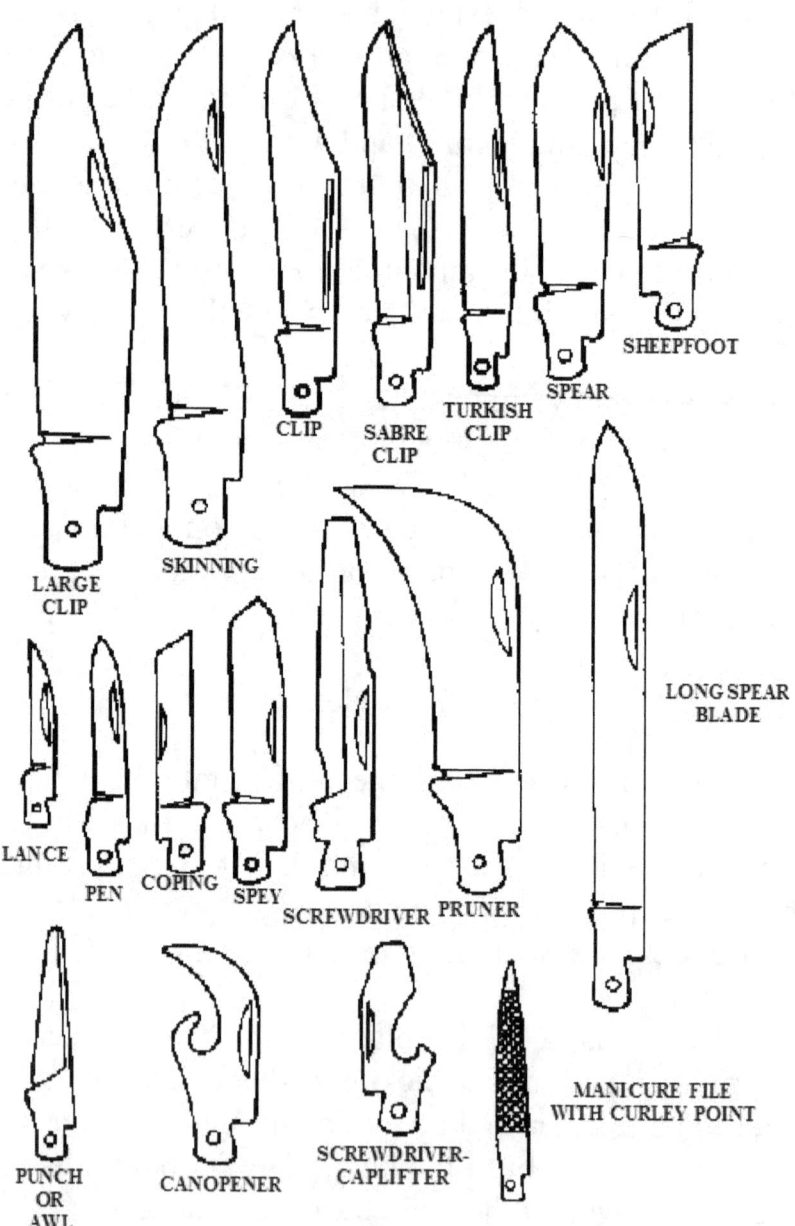

CLIP

SABRE
CLIP

TURKISH
CLIP

SPEAR

SHEEPFOOT

LARGE
CLIP

SKINNING

LANCE

PEN

COPING

SPEY

SCREWDRIVER

PRUNER

LONG SPEAR
BLADE

PUNCH
OR
AWL

CANOPENER

SCREWDRIVER-
CAPLIFTER

MANICURE FILE
WITH CURLEY POINT

The chart shows some basic shapes of pocket knife blades and the industry names given to them.

No matter how many functions or attachments your knife has, the large *main blade* will probably be used more than anything else. None of the blades should ever be used for prying. They are designed for cutting and may break if you use them in any kind of prying, twisting function. Blades angled downward are for skinning and hard cutting jobs. Small, curved blades are for carving. Long thin blades are used in slicing or filleting. Know your knife blade style and shape to understand its main function.

When your knife is not being used, the blade should be closed tightly inside the handle. If your knife blade swings out freely without effort, then your knife is need of repair. The blade on a good quality knife should snap down tightly inside the handle and open smoothly with a click. When the blade is closed in the knife, the edge will stay clean and free from damage. Keep the blade edge clean, sharp, and ready.

A sheath knife or rigid blade knife should always be kept secure in the sheath when not in use. Never swing it around like a sword or throw it. Not only will you damage the knife, you may hurt someone else or yourself.

Blades styles and sizes should fit your intended purpose. There are many different blades or tools that your knife may have. You should read your owners manual, catalog, or instructions that come with the knife to make sure you know how to use each tool on your knife. Each tool or blade should be used properly to be effective and useful.

Basic Tools for Knives

A **can opener** and **bottle opener** are features on many multiple function knives. The **can opener** can be very handy when you are looking at part of your supper in the can in your hand. To use the can opener, poke a hole through the lid next to the rim by catching the under side with the bottom prong of the can opener. With the hook part of the opener, use a rocking motion, pulling the knife very carefully toward you until you have gone all the way around the rim of the can. Be very careful, the edge will be jagged and sharp. Cut the lid off and remove it from the can. Dispose of it quickly in your camp trash bag or can.

The **bottle opener** will usually have a **screwdriver** on the end as well. It will handle most light to medium jobs. The **bottle opener** itself is used for snap-lids on bottles. The bottom of the opener is used to pry the top off the bottle or container. The screwdriver can also be used to open other types of containers, such as small cans with pry open tops. The **bottle opener** tool may also have a **wire stripper**, a small notch on the tool. To strip the vinyl from a wire, determine the amount of insulation to be removed. Carefully score the insulation all the way around. Put the wire end into the notch and hold with your thumb, pulling the vinyl from the wire.

The **philips screwdriver** tool, if your knife has one, is usually located on the back side of the knife and will fold out from the back at a ninety degree angle from the knife. This handy screwdriver is good for light to medium jobs if the handle does not get in the way.

The **awl** is a punch type tool for making small holes in leather, rubber, soft wood, or other materials. It can also be used to make a starter hole for a screw or drill bit. The **awl** will also have a sharp edge for boring a hole in soft wood, leather, or other materials. As the **awl** is turned clockwise, the sharp edge will be bore through the material. Be careful that the **awl** does not close on your hand when turning it to bore the hole.

Some knives will be equipped with a small pair of **scissors**. These are usually not for heavy duty projects but are very handy for small cutting jobs, like string, paper, tape, or materials. Use the scissors with care, they are sharp; be careful folding them back into the knife.

Many knives now have smaller blades with a **serrated edge** or a main blade with a partially **serrated edge**. This blade is for cutting harder materials, such as a small tree limb, meat, cardboard, or rope. These serrated edges are very sharp and usually do not need re-sharpening.

A **sawtooth** blade is a specific blade used for cutting into larger, harder materials like a tree limb or bone in animal in a hunting situation. The blade will have a double or triple row of teeth-like points used for sawing.

A knife for fishing may have a **scaler tool**. This tool is used for scaling the fish you have caught. The tool is scraped along the fish as you hold the tail. This function is pretty specific and usually a specialty knife, or "fish knife" has a **scaler tool** for this purpose.

Smaller pocket knives sometimes have a **manicure nail file** with a point. This tool is for small filing jobs, like your nails, soft wood, jewelry, and the like. Be careful not to demand too much of this small tool.

The **shackle** or hole in the end is for attaching a lanyard of leather, cord, or cotton twine. You may find that you want such a lanyard for hanging your knife, or just for looks. A colored lanyard, made from colored shoe laces, may also help you find your knife in the woods or field if you drop or lose it. Some may use the loop of the lanyard to slip the hand through to hole it while in use – extra care is required to keep from slippage.

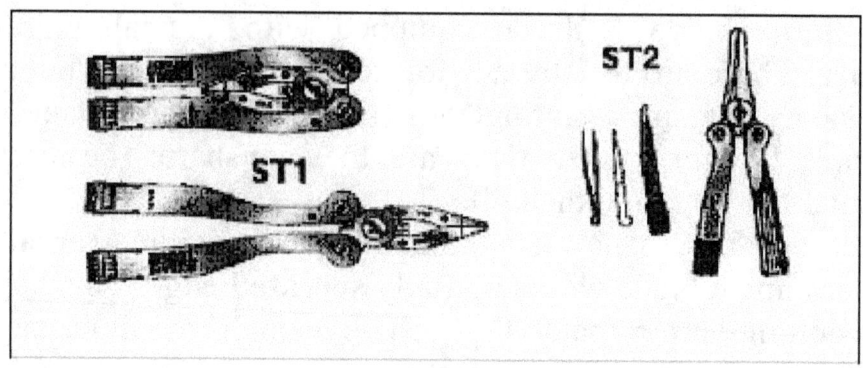

Knife Blade Steel

Knife blades are made of some kind of alloyed steel. The introduction of carbon and other elements during the steel making process makes the steel hard and strong without making it brittle. Carbon-steel can be sharpened easily and the edge will stay sharp a long time. Some knives will be more rust resistant than others due to the alloys in their steel composition. The better made knives are specially hardened and tempered for long life, sharpness, and strength. Keep any knife clean, dry, and lightly oiled to prevent rust.

An excellent steel for knife making is 1095 high carbon steel. The addition of carbon to the steel is necessary for the blade to hold a sharp edge. Stainless steels have a high degree of stain and rust resistance, but are not stain and rust free. The 400 series stainless steel has chrome added to give it the stainless properties and brilliance. Schrade+ stainless steel and other are unique and formulated to give good edge holding characteristics, ease of resharpening, and stain and rust resistance.

When a knife with 1095 steel is new, the blade is nice and shiny. But, high carbon steel, over the course of time, may discolor and turn a grayish tone. This dulling will not change the strength or performance of the knife at all, and is a normal characteristic of the steel used in making the blade. The other tools on the knife will have the same metal properties as the main blade, and equal care must be given to them as well. If your knife has multiple blades, then be sure to check them once in awhile, and keep them clean and free from dirt and residue from your work jobs. Put a small drop of light color machine oil on the ends of the knife where the blades pivot to keep the knife working more smoothly. Wipe off the excess oil with a soft cloth.

Knife Safety Rules

You can never be too safe with a knife. It is not necessary to stress the point that a knife, although it is a tool, can be a very dangerous tool. So, here are the seven basic rules of knife safety that apply to anyone using a knife:

1. A sharp knife is a safe knife.
Keep your knife sharp and clean, free from dirt and grime.
2. Work the blade away from you.
Never pull it toward you or part of your body.
3. Your knife is a hand tool, do not throw it.
Most knives are not designed to throw.
4. Carry your knife with the blade put away.
Fold the knife or put it into the sheath, never carry it open.
5. Never use your knife to chop or hammer or pry.

Chopping, hammering or prying is not your knife's job.

6.   Be aware of the operation of your knife.

Know how it works and have it under your control.

7.   Always use your knife in a safe manner.

Be aware of others and put it away when not in use.

    1.   A sharp knife is a safe knife. A dull knife is a dangerous knife. This is true! A knife that is not sharp is much more a risk than a sharp knife. A dull knife that does not cut and do its job will need more pressure put to it to cut. The chance of an accident is increased when there is more pressure put to bear on the knife. A sharp knife will cut more easily and reduce the chance of an accident. A sharp knife that cuts easily, with less pressure, is a safer knife. A knife is designed to cut. So, if it is sharp, it will do its cutting job much better without hurting you or anyone else near you.

    A sharp knife allows the user to work with less effort and fewer movements of the hands and arm. If the knife is dull, then pressure is put on the knife with more arm muscle and maybe even the other hand, making any situation more risky. A sharp knife will do the best job, and safely.

    2.   Work the blade away from you. Never pull the blade toward you or toward any part of your body. Always consider what might happen if the blade goes into a direction that you were not planning on. If you are pulling the blade toward a part of your body and the knife slips, which it can do, then you may get cut. When you are working with a knife, always be aware of the "blade path". If you are whittling, for instance, consider that the knife blade will leave the stick and flick into the space right in front of you. Make sure that no one is standing there in front of you when you are whittling, carving, or cutting.

The practice of thinking ahead as to "blade path" can be applied to other things like swinging a bat, or using an ax, or turning around with a tool in your hand. This is a matter of awareness of your own "personal space" and the space immediately around you.

3.   Your knife is a hand tool, do not throw it. It is never a good idea to throw your knife. Most importantly, the knife could hurt someone or even you. It can deflect off a surface and bounce back at you or onto someone else.

4.   Carry your knife with the blade put away. Never carry your knife around with the blade open or a rigid blade knife out of its sheath; especially, if you are running, climbing, playing, or even just moving around a campsite. An open blade can be very dangerous if it is in your pocket or dangling from your backpack. If your knife is not in use on a job, then it should be folded up in the handle, or put away in the sheath. If your knife slips open, then it needs to be repaired or replaced. It is not safe and it should be put away until you can tend to it.

5.   Never chop or hammer or pry with your knife. It is not designed to chop, hammer or pry; it is designed to cut. Never strike something with a knife. Never hammer or pound or chop with your knife. A knife is not an ax or hatchet or chisel. The knife can deflect off a log or other object and fly right out of your hand. The knife can also break and cause damage or injury.

6.   Be aware of the operation of your knife. Your knife blade may not be designed to lock open, so you will need to be careful that your hand does not get into a position where the blade can accidently close on it. You would not want to put any kind of pressure on the back of the blade to cause it to begin to close and possibly cause injury.

7. Always use your knife in a safe manner and put it away when it is not in use. Be very aware when there are others around you. You must remember your own "personal space" and the space you will take up using the knife. Be aware of the "blade path", or follow through angle of the knife when cutting. If the knife accidentally slips, you want to know where it will be going. If someone is in the way, then change your position to keep safe.

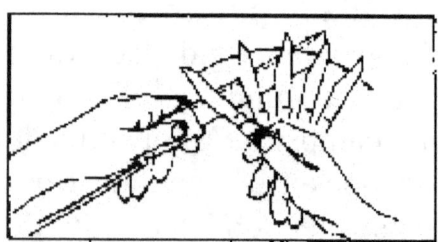 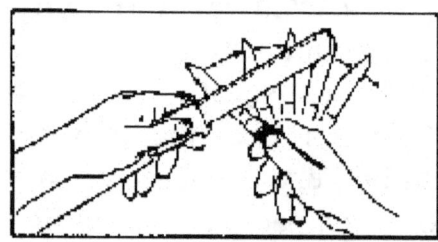

Hold Honesteel or sharpening stone with rounded edge up. Sharpen blade by using a sweeping motion, sliding blade about one inch from sheath handle to end of Honesteel. Repeat this procedure on the bottom of Honesteel as if you were using a butcher's steel.

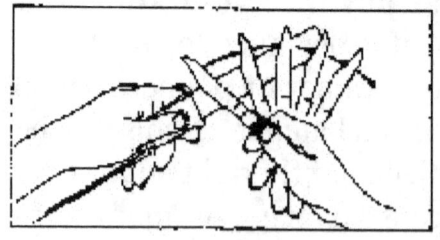 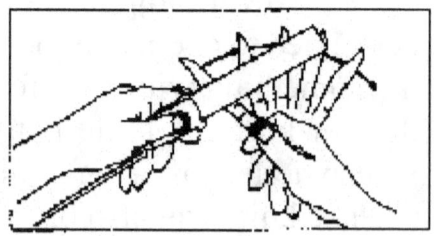

Finish sharpening blade by turning the Honesteel or stone and bring blade across the flat side alternating this motion from top to bottom as if you were using a butcher's steel.

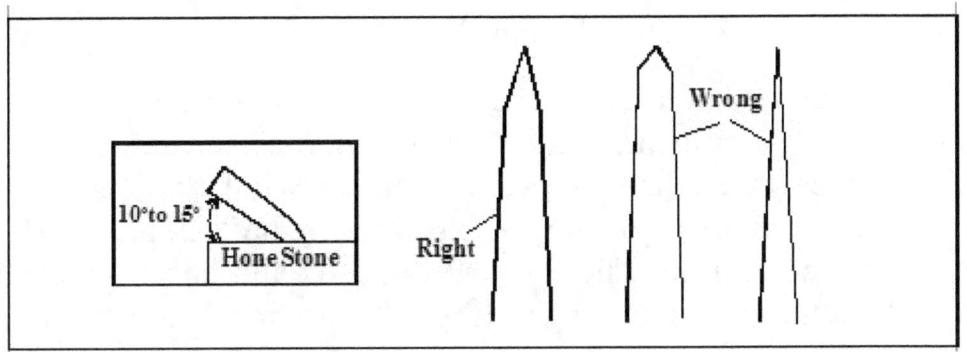

Here are the rules of knife safety again:

1. A sharp knife is a safe knife.
   Keep your knife sharp and clean, no dirt and grime.

2. Work the blade away from you.
   Never pull it toward you or part of your body.

3. Your knife is a hand tool, do not throw it.
   Your knife is not designed to throw.

4. Carry your knife with the blade put away.
   Fold it or put it into the sheath, never carry it open.

5. Never use your knife to chop or hammer or pry.
   Chopping or hammering is not your knife's job.

6. Be aware of the operation of your knife.
   Know how it works and have it under your control.

7. Always use your knife in a safe manner.
   Be aware of others and put it away when not in use.

Basic Parts of a Pocket Knife

A standard folding pocket knife with three blades and about three to four inches long can have up to 22 separate parts. Better knives, like Schrade knives and others, will have over 100 hand operations that go into the making of the "simple", yet intricate pocket knife. There are inspections and check points throughout the manufacturing process of better made knives that insure quality, safety,   and reliability.

The basic parts of a pocket knife are useful to know. The main part, of course, is the *blade*. The *blade* may be any one of many different basic styles; and, it is designed to cut. Each style blade is designed with some special feature or task in view. So, each blade style has a basic purpose for its design.

The outside part that you hold in your hand is simply called the *handle (or handles)*. Handle materials will vary. The handles are held secure to the knife with *pins* and *rivets*. The end pieces (if they are on the knife), which are usually brass or a polished silver/nickel metal, are called *bolsters*. The handle material in this type of construction covers the entire knife and the *bolsters* are riveted securely to the *linings*. Some knives have special *handles* that do not require *bolsters* and the handle material runs the full length of the knife.

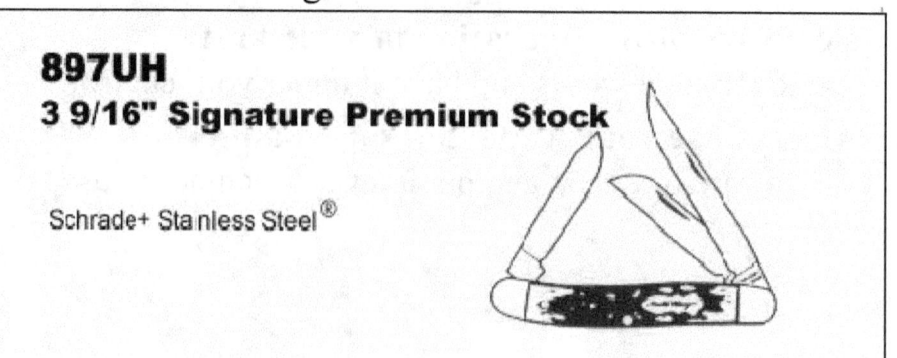

897UH
3 9/16" Signature Premium Stock

Schrade+ Stainless Steel®

Parts of a Pocket Knife

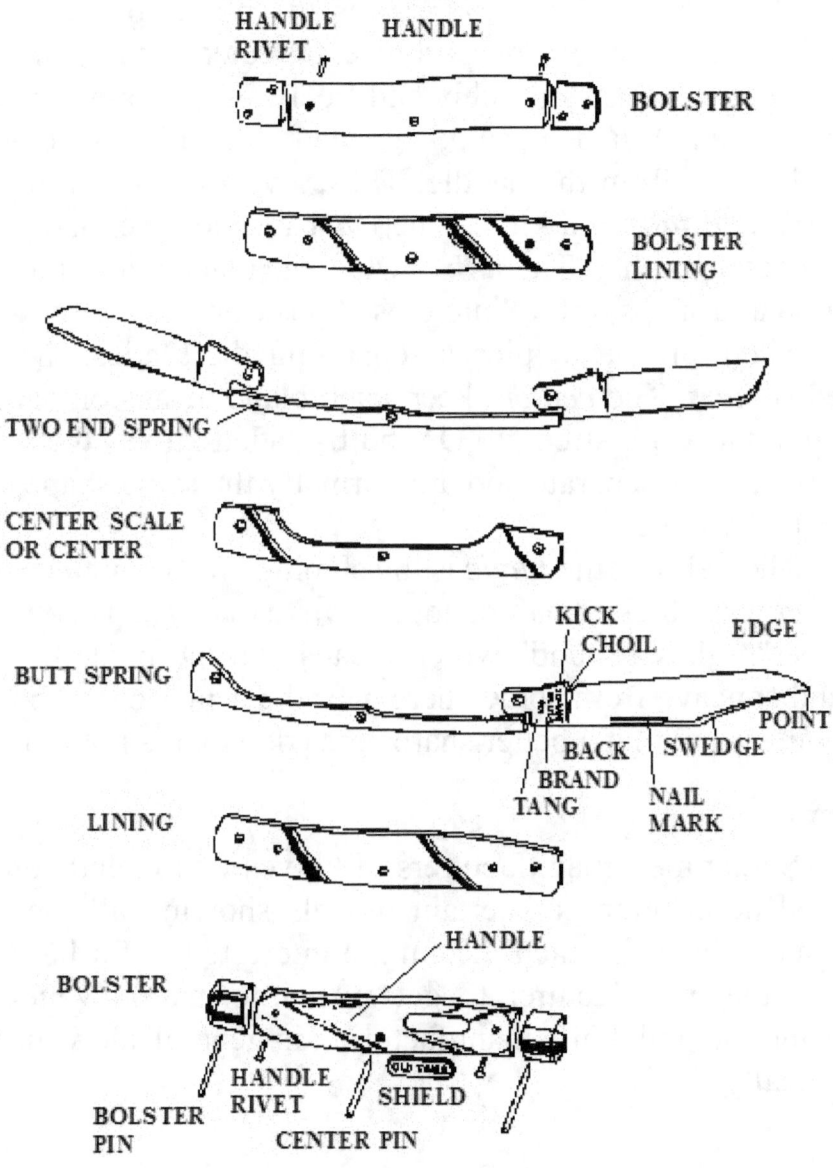

HANDLE RIVET   HANDLE   BOLSTER

BOLSTER LINING

TWO END SPRING

CENTER SCALE OR CENTER

BUTT SPRING   KICK   CHOIL   EDGE

POINT

BACK   SWEDGE

BRAND TANG   NAIL MARK

LINING

HANDLE

BOLSTER

HANDLE RIVET   SHIELD

BOLSTER PIN   CENTER PIN

OLD TIMER

SCHRADE OLD TIMER 8OT

19

The blades or tools swing out of the knife and snap back into the knife because of the piece of metal along the back side, called the *spring*. The *spring* keeps the blade in the open or closed position. When properly heat treated, the *spring* will make the *blade* open smoothly and freely and snap into position when opened. When closing, the blade should snap closed a short distance from the handle. These two functions are called the **walk** and **talk** of a knife. The **walk** is when the blade opens and closes smoothly. The **talk** is when the blade clicks into open position and snaps tightly into closed position.

There are metal pieces separating the blades, these are called *centers*. The *centers* keep each blade in its compartment and give the knife strength. On multi-bladed knives the *centers* keep the blades separate and are normally the same shape as the *liners* and *handle*.

The *bevel* of the *blade* is the sloping area from the back of the *blade*, the thickest part on top, down to the *edge*. Blade *bevels* may be "hollow ground" which means that the blade has been ground concave from somewhere near the center of the blade to the *edge*, providing a better sharpened edge that is not too thick.

NOTE:

Sometimes, manufacturers of knives will include or offer detailed descriptions of certain models showing all the many parts and names for each. If you are interested in further study, contact the manufacturer to get such information which will acquaint you with knife manufacturing in general and your knife specifically.

Rigid Blade Shapes

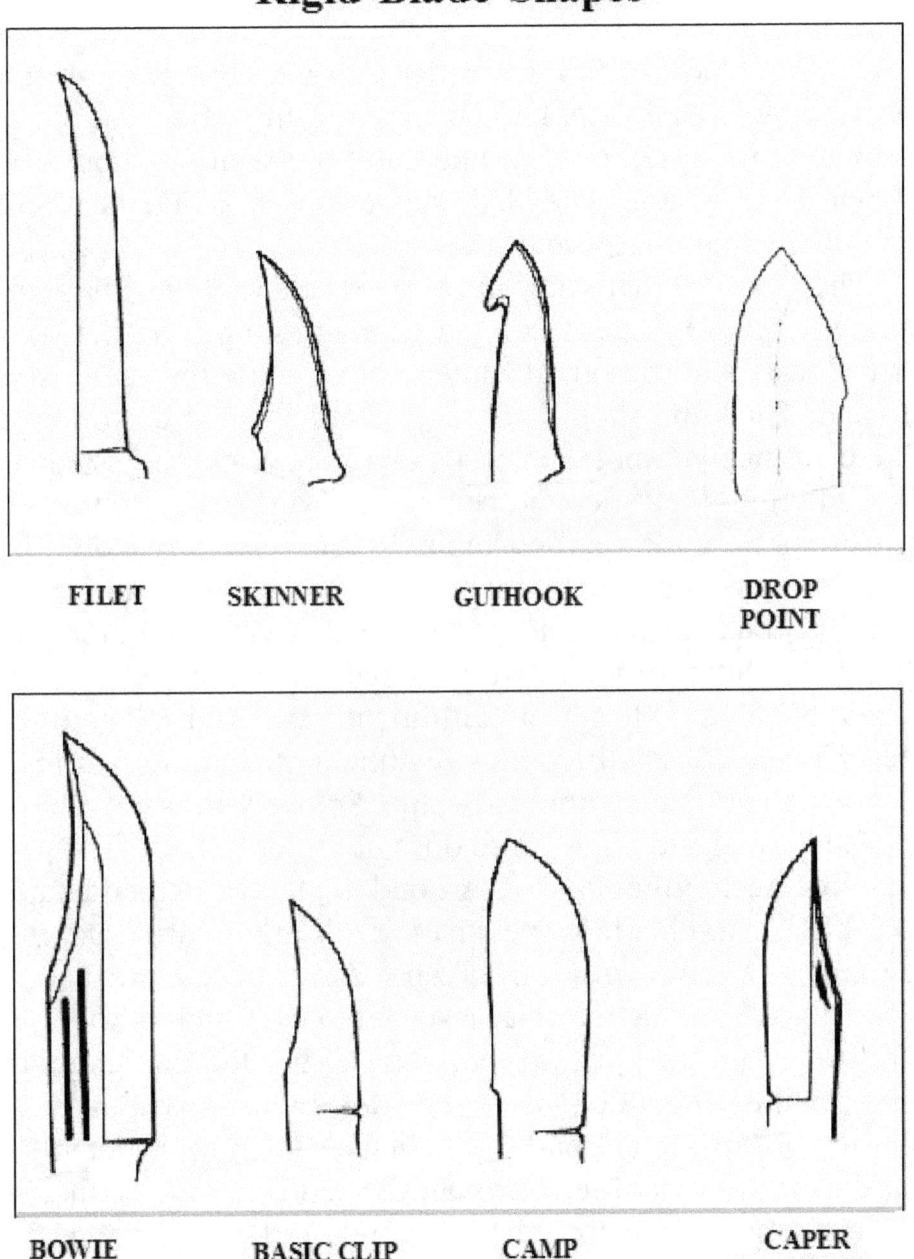

FILET   SKINNER   GUTHOOK   DROP POINT

BOWIE   BASIC CLIP   CAMP   CAPER or CLIP

The Basic Rigid Blade Knife

A rigid blade knife (also called a straight blade or sheath knife) is a very useful tool for camp or home. Because these knives are usually larger, extreme care and caution should be taken when using them. The blade shape, size, and thickness will determine the main purpose of the knife.

The handle material on a rigid blade knife is very important to your usage. Pick a material and shape that fits your hand well and allows you absolute control while the knife is in your hand. The knife should not feel "handle heavy" as you hold it. There are many handle materials on the market today such as rubber, fiberglass, plastic, and composites (a good example of a composite is Schrade's unbreakable "staglon"). Care should be taken as to the claims of offshore manufacturers--the materials may not be high caliber and quality. The style and color you choose are a matter of your own personal preferences.

The rigid blade knife has been traditionally called the "Hunting Knife". Knives are so varied now that the term "hunting knife" has lost some of its meaning and value. So, we will use the term rigid blade. The rigid blade knife does not fold up, the *blade* and *handle* are one continuous unit. A good quality rigid blade knife (like Schrade rigid blade knives) have full *tang* or thru *tang* construction. A knife with full *tang* has a one piece *blade* and *handle* with the handle material fastened to each side of the handle steel. The steel in a thru *tang* knife runs the full length of the knife and is embedded inside the *handle*. Less expensive knives will insert a small part of the blade steel into the handle rather than running the steel through the handle for strength.

The first thing to consider in a good rigid blade knife is the balance. The knife should feel good in the hand so that there is proper weight distribution between the *blade* and the *handle*. The downward motion of the knife should feel very natural to you as you hold it.

The main part of the *blade* is the *edge*, the part you cut with. The entire *handle* section of the knife is called the *hilt*. On the *hilt* is found the *pommel*, or *butt*. The *pommel* may be a separate piece of metal or other material attached to the end of the *handle*. There may also be a separate piece of metal between the *handle* and the *blade* called the *guard*. The *guard* keeps your hand away from the *edge* of the *blade* when working with the knife. Some of theses guard may be very decorative, and some may be merely part of the handle shape. Brass is usually the metal of choice in the traditional "hunting" knives.

Taking Care of Your Knife

Your knife will always be ready when you need it if you keep it in good condition. When you come back in from a camping or fishing trip and your knife needs some work, get right to it so it will be ready the next time you want to use it. Always keep your knife clean from dirt, mud, rust, and debris of any kind. If your knife gets wet for any reason, dry it off thoroughly. You may use a light oil (like household lubricant, light machine oil, or spray-on lubricants) to wipe over the blades and tools and to put on the hinged parts. Make sure you wipe off any excess oil.

Whenever your knife will be in storage for a long time, be sure to put a light coating of oil on the blades and ends. This will help to keep it from rusting. Knives that have real brass ends should not be stored in the leather sheath without some kind of tissue paper or plastic around the brass to keep it from touching

Parts of a Rigid Blade Knife

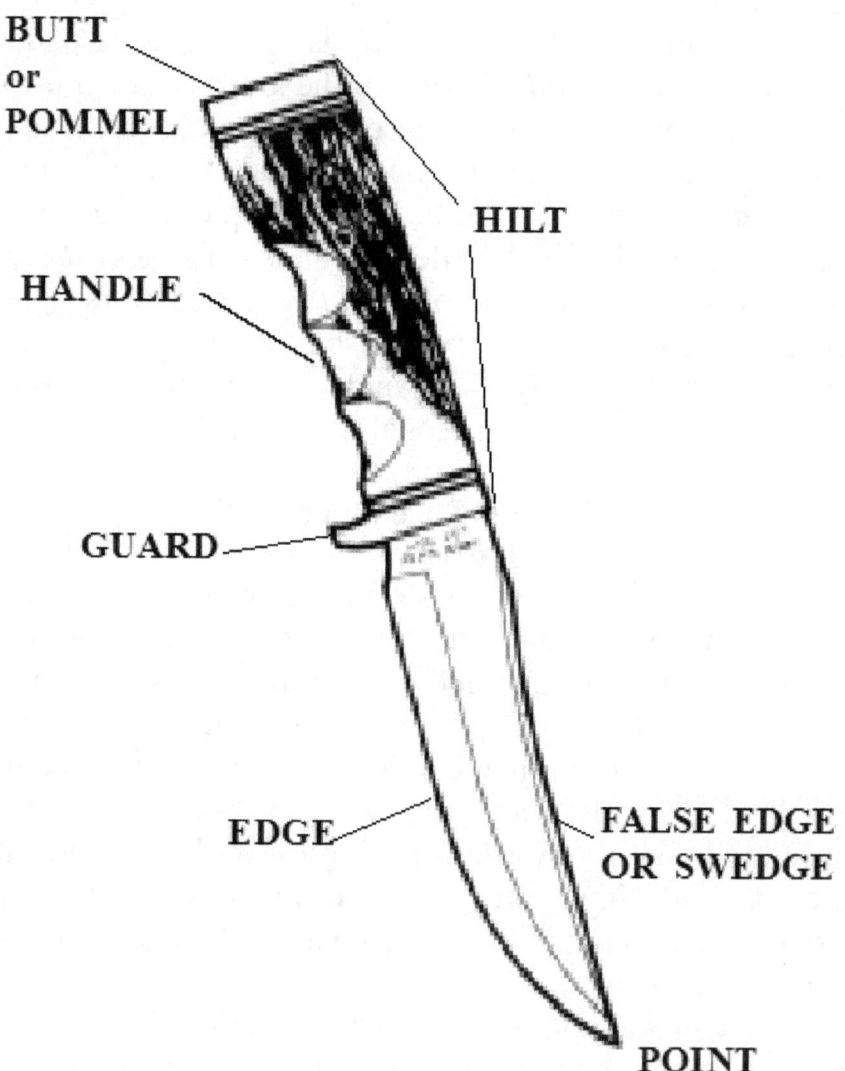

BUTT
or
POMMEL

HILT

HANDLE

GUARD

EDGE

FALSE EDGE
OR SWEDGE

POINT

Schrade 153UH Golden Spike

the leather. Sheaths made of other materials will not harm the knife, but the leather of some sheaths may cause the brass to discolor and turn a greenish color. This discoloration can be removed with a number of cleaning products on the market, including mild chrome polish and environment safe tarnish removers.

Be careful with rigid blade knives (straight bladed knives) when they are stored. If they have a brass guard and are in a leather sheath, then wrap them with a tissue paper or plastic to keep the brass from contacting the leather. If the knife handle is rubber or some other synthetic material, it is not necessary to wrap. It is still a good idea to put a light oil coating on the blade before storing the knife for any length of time.

When displaying your knife, whether it is a rigid blade or pocket knife, turn it to show the "front display side", which is the side that shows the *tang stamp*. The folding knife should be pointing to the observer's right, *blade* partially open or up on an angle from the handle with the back of the knife down. A straight or rigid blade should be pointed to the observer's right, *blade edge* down.

Knife Sheath Care

Sheaths need special care and maintenance. You may experience some unraveling with the nylon and the new hi-tech sheaths. With a small knife blade or tweezers or finger nail file tip, gently push the threads back into the hole; then, put a small dab of super glue gel into the hole and let dry. These sheaths must be kept clean and dry and free from dirt and mud. A gentle washing with liquid dish washing soap will not damage the fibers of the sheath. The new hi-tech materials, which are a thickly woven material or leathers can also be glued with a super glue gel or a bonding glue. Carefully, you may use a fine point soldering tool for nylon sheaths to lightly touch the torn spot or repair area. The materials in the high tech sheaths will melt with high heat, thus creating the bonding for a repair. If gluing two pieces that have come apart, use a small clamp or clip to hold in place until dry. You may also use small two part rivets or "Chicago screws" to repair leather or thickly woven materials. A "Chicago screw" is a small screw with a threaded sleeve. The sleeve goes through the hole like a rivet, but a screw is used to anchor and hold.

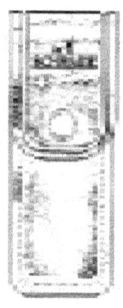 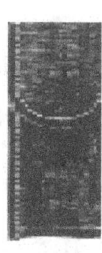  

Leather sheaths must be kept clean and free from dirt. Dirt is the number one enemy of leather products of any kind, including knife sheaths. Dirt will ruin the finish, make the sheath hard, crack the surface, and may even destroy the stitching. It is a good idea to oil your leather sheath when you think it needs it. If it appears to be dry and cracked, or just a bit brittle, you may consider rubbing some oil into the leather. Pure neatsfoot oil (not neatsfoot compound) is a good leather conditioner. There are many good leather conditioner products on the market that are useful with leather sheaths. If your sheath is dirty, then clean it first. Use water and a good saddle soap or glycerin bar to clean the leather before you oil it. Remember to always allow the leather to dry before you apply oil.

A mild solution of dish washing liquid and water will also clean a leather sheath. The sheath must be completely dry before oil is rubbed in. The color of the sheath will darken when you rub oil into the leather. The darkening of the leather is a mark of aging and is normally considered nice looking. If you object to the darkening, then find a light oil product that will not darken the leather. You can find good leather cleaning and conditioning products at shoe repair shops, horse tack shops, farm and feed stores, some hardware stores, and discount department stores.

The most important thing to remember with leather is to keep it clean. Too much oil may rot the stitching, so be careful to do only what is necessary to maintain the good condition of your sheath.

Knife Sharpening

Remember that the very first rule of knife safety is that a "sharp knife is a safe knife". When you have used your knife and you determine that it needs sharpening, do it as soon as you are able so that it will be sharp the next time you use it. It is a simple thing to get your knife sharp and keep it sharp. If your knife has sustained some damage, then it must be repaired by someone who knows how. Nicks and chips in the cutting edge can be dangerous and they lessen the usefulness of the knife. In this case you may want to send your knife back to the manufacturer to have it repaired. Some breaks (like the very tip breaking off the blade) can be overlooked for a time and the knife will still be quite usable until you have a chance to repair it or send it into the factory for repair or replacement. Many facilities repair and sharpen knives these days. You may find hardware stores, feed stores and sharpening shops that will repair knives .

There are many sharpening products on the market today but they all do basically the same thing: grind the edge of the blade down to create a sharp edge. There are diamond dusted small slabs of metal, Arkansas stones in all kinds of shapes and sizes, oil stones with one side coarse and one side smooth, steel honing sticks, metal rods, and on and on.

A very good sharpening system is a honesteel with two surfaces to sharpen the blade surface, the edge for sharpening, and the flat surface for fine finishing. Some of these products have a leather sheath that turns into a handle when sharpening.

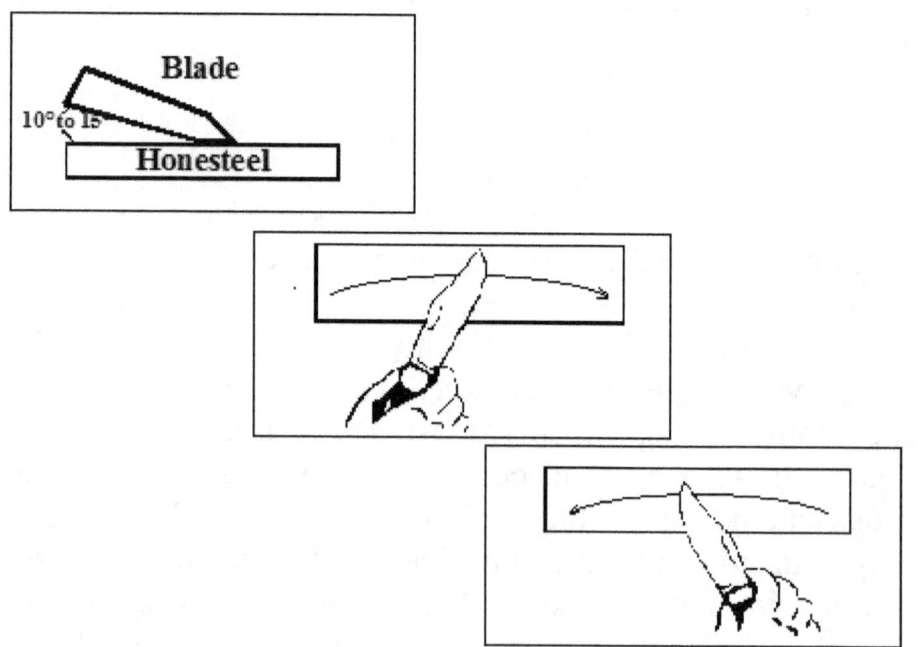

You will not get a good sharp edge unless some of the blade steel is removed by sharpening. So, some kind of stone or honesteel may be best to start your sharpening maintenance. The method is to stroke the edge of the blade over the stone or steel, evenly, as if you were "cutting" or "slicing" the stone or steel.

This method moves the edge of the blade over the stone or steel, in an even manner. The knife should be held at about a 10 to 15 degree angle as you move it across the cutting surface of the sharpening device you are using, in a slicing or shaving motion (see illustration).

As the blade edge is scraped over the stone or steel, metal is being removed and with each stroke the blade becomes a little sharper. "Shave" the knife blade away from your body across the stone or steel, as if you were slicing it. In just a few strokes the edge will become sharper. Finish the job with a finer stone or steel. On most stones, you will wet them with water or a special honing oil. The water or oil will carry the particles left by the sharpening process away and off the stone. When finished, just wash and wipe the stone clean. Some stones have two surfaces, a coarse surface for sharpening and a fine surface for finishing.

The sharpening steels or honesteels, whether a stick or a rod, do not need water or oil. Wipe the steel clean with a soft cloth after usage. The same angle is used on the steels   as on the stones. Some honesteels may have four sharpening surfaces; rounded edges for sharpening, and flat surfaces for finishing on both sides of the steel.

Small rectangular shaped stones are available for sharpening, like the ones that come on the sheaths of larger rigid knives. These are handy small stones to take with you into the outdoors. They are great to use in a field situation. Hold the knife securely in one hand and pass the stone across the edge of the blade, using small circular motions. The experienced knife user might hold a small stone on edge and sharpen with the "slicing" motion.

Wetting sharpening stones with water will make the job go faster and keep the stone free from debris and metal. If you have a small stone for use at home, glue it or clamp it down to a board to give you something to hold onto. Or you may mount a small wooden frame on the board to hold the stone in place. Holding the knife securely and using small circular motions, or holding the stone on edge using the slicing motion works just as well at home as it does in the outdoors.

Check your knife sharpness by brushing or lightly scraping your finger over the edge of the blade perpendicular to the edge. Never run your finger up and down the edge of a blade, or you will cut yourself. You may also try to "shave" the corner of a small piece of paper by cutting it downward to see if your knife will cut it. Hold the paper securely and cut downward on the stiff edge nearer your hand.

Some knives may have special procedures or special ways of sharpening them. It is always a good idea to check with the instructions that come with the knife to see what the manufacturer suggests on the sharpening of the blade. It is also true that some knives need sharpening only on one side, and others do not need sharpening at all, such as the serrated blades on the new hi-tech knives. If you are ever in doubt as to the process to sharpen your knife, contact the manufacturer.

Some manufacturers include a guide to sharpening with their knives and a brief commentary as to your warranty information. If you need any other information, call or write to the address listed. There are many publications produced to help you get the most out of your knives for years of trouble free use.

Outdoor Camping & Hiking Tips

1)   Wet matches do not start fires. Paint the tips of your matches with finger nail polish to waterproof them. Put them in a plastic snack bag, or a match carrier available at most camping or department stores. Consider carrying a lighter, or even a refillable lighter, as a back up to the matches, or as a main light. After all, why fight the matches when a small portable lighter will do the job?

2)   Small "one match" charcoal briquettes can get a friendly fire going. Five or six of them can also be used for a small breakfast fire that is easy to put out and will not waste wood. If the charcoal is not burned up, it can be used later in the day to start another fire.

3)   For roasting marshmallows or cooking hot dogs, be sure to use green sticks from nearby bushes. Cut what you need from the bottom of a bush. Then, soak the ends of the sticks in water for an hour or so to keep them from catching on fire.

4)   A great food snack for a camping or hiking trip is to cut the core out of an apple and fill the cored apple with your favorite peanut butter. You may want to add raisins to the peanut butter.

5)   Ever tried to start a fire in the rain? Every part of the country has tinder that will burn. The great cedars of the North, the tall pines of the West, and the cypress of the South, will all burn when wet. To help the tinder get going, stuff it into a waxed paper cup, then light the cup. Put dry kindling on top of the burning cup. Next time, keep your wood under cover, if you are able. Dryer lint from your home clothes dryer works well, too

(yes, it does). Raid the lent trap from the home dryer and put in small plastic bags. It will light for an easy to get tinder. Stuff it into a small wax paper cup and your fire is soon ready.

6)	For a small cook fire, use only the wood you need. Build a small tepee shaped fire, then light it. When you put your finger sized wood on the burning fire, crisscross the sticks and let the flames burn down a bit, then you are ready with a cook fire that will last long enough to cook your food. Add small amounts of wood as needed.

7)	Before cooking over an open fire, rub the bottoms of your pans and pots with bar soap. The soot will wash off more easily. Keeping pots and pans clean out in the field is very important to your health and well-being on an outdoor trip. Practically, being sick due to unclean habits does not a happy camper make.

8)	To get stubborn food out of a dirty pan, use coffee grounds, dirt or sand to rub out the food particles stuck to the pan or pot; then, wash with water and soap.

9)	A small hole in the ground lined with a piece of heavy plastic will make a terrific wash basin for doing your dishes or even a small load of laundry. Two holes will provide one basin for washing and one for rinsing.
10)	A pencil lead is made of graphite, a dry lubricant. You can use a pencil to rub over the zipper track on a stubborn sleeping bag, pants, or jacket. Rubbing a candle over the zipper track works well as a lubricant, if you remembered to bring a candle.

11)	Anytime you are in the woods, it is a good idea to stay

away from any plant with three leaves. Poison Ivy will grow on the ground and in vines up a tree. If you come in contact with Poison Ivy, Poison Oak, or Poison Sumac, wash with soap and warm water as soon as possible to help stop the spreading. "Leaves of three, let them be." Learn these plants and what they look like, and stay away!

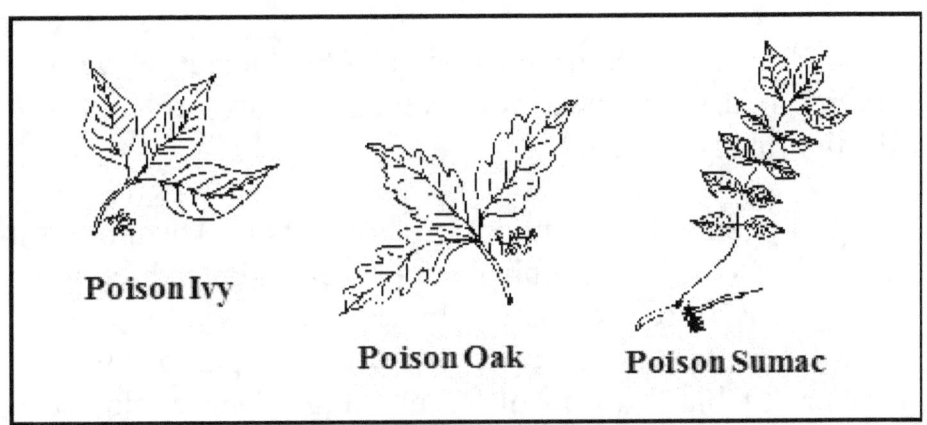

Poison Ivy

Poison Oak

Poison Sumac

12)   An inexpensive box of baking soda is good to have on any outdoor trip. You can use it to sprinkle on your hands for a better grip on something slimy or wet; sprinkle it in your boots to help keep your feet dry from sweat; store it in the cooler to help absorb odors; help wash your dishes and drinking equipment; add it to your rinse water for pots, pans, dishes, and clothes; and, if you forget your toothpaste, you can brush your teeth with baking soda.

13)   If you want eggs and toast for breakfast but do not like the way the eggs spread all over the pan, eat a hole in the bread first. Then, put the bread in the pan and drop the egg inside the hole in the bread. Cook to taste. You can also add cheese or other veggie ingredients that you might brought with you – a camper's omelet.

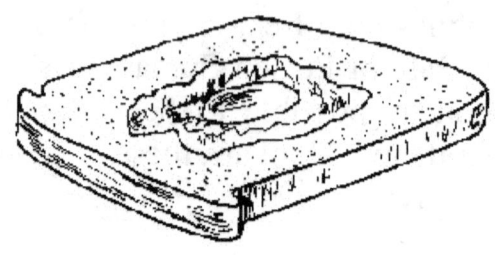

14)   A gas lantern or camp stove is not a tent heater. Never use these items to dry and heat your tent. Not only are they fire hazards, the fumes are deadly.

15)   A good item on any outdoor trip is a whistle. The universal code for being lost is the number three of anything. Three fires, three car horns, three yells, or three blasts from your little whistle. You can work out a code with your companions where the numbers of blasts mean different things. One could mean "where are you?", two could mean "come quick!" and so on.

16)   If you are hiking, you need not take a large grill. There are very small gas stoves on the market that you can purchase. Or, a metal grill top or a few steel rods can be used as a grill for your pans and pots over a small fire. Weight and packing will be cut to a minimum, which is an important factor when hiking or camping.

17)   Always carry an assortment of plastic bags, all sizes and all kinds. Shopping bags make great garbage bags and food bags for storage. Small sandwich bags are good for a host of things for storage and travel, including parts, various travel kits, supplies, and small quantity items. Small plastic jars are good for food stuffs, too. Avoid glass jars and bottles because they could break.

18)   Put a few grains of rice in your camp salt shaker to keep the salt from clumping do to moisture.

19)   Do not fry food in an aluminum pan; the food will most assuredly stick. Take a small teflon pan, or if weight is not a problem, you will enjoy a cast iron skillet or pan. If you use a small aluminum or steel pan, be sure to add some non-stick additive to keep food from sticking.

20)   Large 8 inch or 10 inch nails, found in hardware stores, are terrific tent stakes and are not as bulky as the larger plastic stakes that come with the tent. If weight is a problem, such as on a hiking trip, lightweight aluminum rods with the ends bent over work very nicely; or, the style of tent may not even need stakes. Your body weight will hold it down, or rope tied to trees will replace stakes. See   drawings on tents in this section.

21)   No one knife will do everything. Consider taking a few knives to do the intended tasks for your trip. Your cooking/kitchen knife, hanging on the tree next to the table, will be a better choice than pulling your pocket knife out to slice some food. A few smaller knives will be a lot better than one great big one. Choose knives with different blade styles to suit different tasks. It is better to have a couple of extras than to be missing what you need.

22)   Most of the time a full ax is not needed in camp; wood is plentiful on the ground. A full length ax is usually not a necessary item. But, take a small ax with a "Michigan head" style and cut the handle down from its 30 inches to 14 or 15 inches; or, replace the ax handle with a large hatchet handle. Then, you will have a "hatchet" that will do a lot more than most hatchets. The following chart illustrates some of the basic ax shapes.

23)   Tie bright colored lanyards on anything and everything you can of your equipment. The lanyards can help by providing something in which to hang that piece of gear. And, if something gets lost or misplaced, it will be easier to find in the outdoors because of the bright colors.

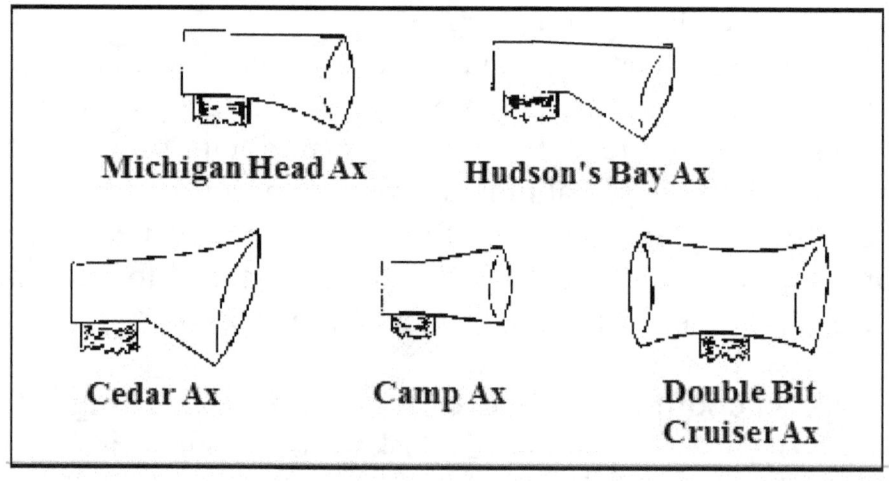

Michigan Head Ax   Hudson's Bay Ax

Cedar Ax   Camp Ax   Double Bit
                                   Cruiser Ax

24)   Always carry more socks than you think you will need. A good practice is two pair more than the days out. Dry socks can make a happier camper in the rain.

25)   As to your pack, it is always a good idea to put clothing

and bulkier, larger items toward the outside of the pack and to the center of the back; softer items lower in the pack. Put heavier items toward the top at your shoulders.

26)   Frozen leftovers or pre-prepared frozen meals packed in the cooler are great meals with little preparation.

27)   Foil dinners are fun to make and are easy to prepare out in the field. Be sure to layer your slices of food (whatever it is: butter, potatoes, onions, burger, fish, chicken, vegetables), season it from layer to layer, double the foil wrap, and be sure to seal the pouch air tight. Just before you seal up the last end, put up to about a third of a cup of water in the pouch. Your food will not stick to the foil and it will cook faster.

28)   A lightweight fishing vest makes a great camping or hiking outer garment because of all of the pockets and places to put things that you want accessible.

29)   When building a large fire for the evening, use the larger logs at the bottom, laying the logs in layers, one layer with the logs one way, and the next layer crisscrossed the other way. Go up about four or five layers, then build your small fire on top. The fire will last the evening as it burns down through the layers.

30)   Small pieces of leather or laces can be strung through the eyelets of zippers on packs and equipment making it easier to find the zippers. Tie the leather or lace onto the zipper, or make a small loop and tie a knot. Leather laces and pieces of leather can be purchased at most farm and feed stores. For a modest sum you will get a bundle of leather laces for uses at home and camp.

Tepee Fire
Burns quickly
for cooking fires

Star Fire
Push in logs
as they burn

Reflector Fire
For heating
and roasting

31)   When packing food for a trip, use waxed paper between layers of foods, like meat, cheese, and vegetables. The food will not stick together, you will have a preparation surface, and the used waxed paper can be used as kindling to start your next fire.

32)   If you want fresh eggs but are afraid to take them on a trip, break them into a baby food jar, or a small plastic jar from instant coffee or other food products. There are egg carrying products that you can purchase, but the baby food jars are more fun.

33)   On a camping trip, a small bucket is a handy piece of gear to have with you. It can be used for packing up things. It is also a sink, a wash basin, a water carrier, and a personal clean up utility.

34)   Learn some basic knots and have plenty of different sizes of rope with you on any trip. The right knot in the right application will save you a lot of grief. Consult scout manuals, camping books, climbing manuals, and general outdoor guides to

find out about good knots. Knowing a few good knots will help you and keep your gear and projects secured. Drawings of basic knots and how to tie them can be found in many outdoor publications.

---

10 BASIC KNOTS TO LEARN AND KNOW
square, sheep shank, half hitch, bowline, double bowline, overhand, sheet bend, figure eight, clove hitch, taut-line hitch

---

35)   Even if you are not accustomed to wearing a hat, wear one in the woods. You will be protected from tree sap, bird droppings, sun, rain, and other elements of the outdoors. The hat will decrease heat loss through your head and insulate your head to keep you warmer in the colder weather; but, it will also keep you cooler in warm weather, insulating your head from the extreme, direct heat of the sun, thereby protecting you.

36)   Make sure that when your flashlights are stored between trips, take out the batteries and keep them in the fridge, or a cold, dry place. They will be fresher when you load them up for your next trip out.

37)   A good sized tarpaulin can be used to build a canopy, a tent, equipment cover, sleeping bag outer layer, tent cover in extreme rainy conditions, and tent under layer.

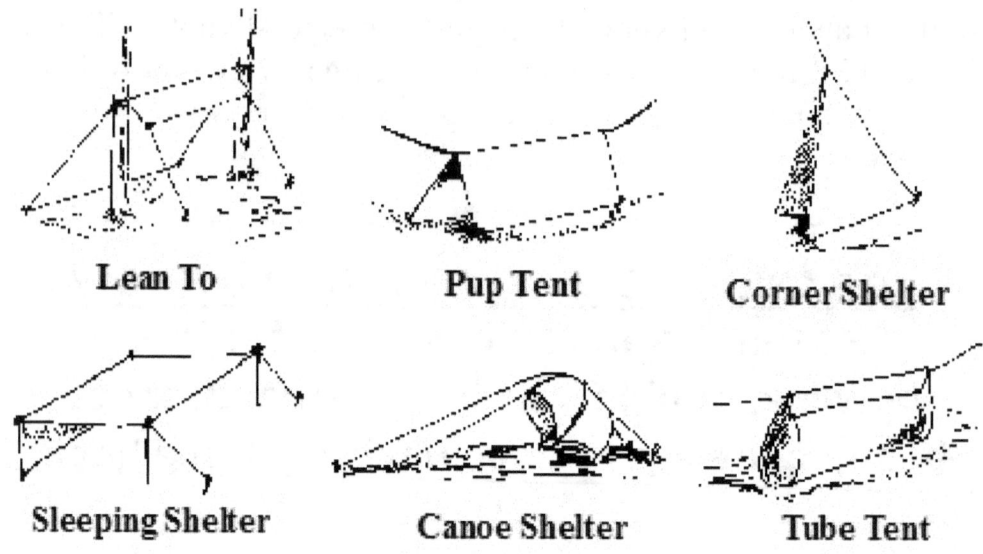

Lean To   Pup Tent   Corner Shelter

Sleeping Shelter   Canoe Shelter   Tube Tent

38)   When cooking a hot dog over an open fire, run the stick into one end of the hot dog, and through the center, so that it will not spin over the fire.

39)   Layer your clothes in cold weather rather than wearing one or two large, thick garments. Layering allows you to regulate your body temperature by putting on and taking off the layers as the weather warms or cools, so you can remain comfortable at any temperature. Less bulky clothes are also easier to pack.

40)   If you forget your bug repellant on your next camping trip, try to stop the use of your sprays and colognes. Stand in the smoke of the fire for awhile and turn around until your clothes are filled with the smoke. The bugs do not like it almost as much as you do not.

41)   Always pack a pair of work gloves. Leather gloves are best for protection from all the things that can hurt you when doing chores. In many parts of the country, small critters and snakes are likely to be lurking about and may be in the next wood pile you put your hand into.

42)   There is no need to pack an entire tube of toothpaste for a one to three night camping trip. Just squeeze a small amount of paste into the corner of a sandwich bag, slip the toothbrush in with the paste and seal it up.

43)   Empty gallon milk jugs are terrific water pots for keeping water at a campsite. Wash them out thoroughly and carry them empty or filled to your camp. Smaller jugs can be used for mixing juices and other drinks at camp.

44)   When not using or preparing food, put the food away and seal it properly in plastic bags or containers. This practice keeps insects, bugs, rodents, and in some areas, large animals out of your meal food. In many parts of the country, animals are pretty adept at getting to the food, so secure it or hang it from limbs so animals will not get to it. Never leave open food in a tent or camp area.

45)   Build your own first aid kit or buy a ready-made kit, but always take a first aid kit with you on an outdoor trip and know how to use its contents.

Basic First Aid Kit Items

Sterilized Gauze Squares, assorted sizes

Gauze on a roll, two or three inch & Safety pins

Bandages with dressing, assorted sizes

Adhesive medical tape, one half to one inch wide

Pair of small scissors & Pair of tweezers

Wooden applicator sticks & Q-tips

Antibiotic ointment & Tube of lubricant

Soap or cleansing agent

Aspirin or substitute for fever reduction

Bottle of Alcohol & Bottle of Hydrogen Peroxide

First Aid Book (Scouts or Red Cross)

Notes:

Outdoor Manners

Any time you are on an outdoor trip, whether it is camping, hunting, fishing, climbing, hiking, boating, canoeing, or just nature walking, you are a guest. You are in another habitat. It is your responsibility to treat the outdoors with respect and care. No one will take care of it if you do not; and, that is the attitude to take and keep.

The way you act and behave outdoors is a reflection of the kind of person you are. You will want to respect the outdoors and all that is in it. If you have good manners at home, then you will want to carry your good manners with you into the outdoors.

If your manners need improvement, then the outdoors is a good opportunity to practice. It may sound like fun to carve your name into the smooth bark of a birch tree; but, you may be opening a wound in that tree that could cause an infection that would destroy that tree and maybe other trees around it.

Outdoor manners have to do with showing respect for others and their property, obeying the laws of the area you are in, leaving clean campsites when you depart, and not polluting waterways and woods with litter and garbage. Stay on the designated trails and pathways to prevent added erosion and wildlife damage. Each of us doing our part will help keep our outdoor experiences good ones. It really is true that if all of us are more mindful of the outdoor areas that we like to go to, and if we take care of those areas; then, the environment will begin to get better and better, little by little.

"Leave only footprints, take only pictures."

Conservation & the Environment

We live in a society that is very conscious of the environment and keeping the world a nice place to live. You will always want to leave an outdoor area in better shape than when you arrived. Fire safety is a top priority. You will always need to be sure that campfires are out and covered over. As much as possible, use firewood that you find on the ground laying around. It is very easy to find enough wood for a whole trip just lying on the ground from downed trees in the area. Never throw your trash and refuse in a stream or body of water. It will not go away, it will end up somewhere else and someone else will have to clean it up-- having to clean up your outdoor mess.

Many organizations are committed to the well being of the environment. You may want to contact some of these organizations to see what you can do to help. Community organizations, outdoor clubs, scouts, sportsman's clubs, and public conservation clubs in your state or county are all involved in helping to keep America clean and beautiful.

There are also some organizations that are working to save certain habitats of animals and birds. You may want to work on a school or organization project having to do with the conservation or the ecology of a local area. When you have assignments for writing or speaking, you may want to pick an environmental issue and research it, write about it, speak about it. There are many things you can do. When you go camping, bring your trash home. Do not try to burn tin cans and foil wrappings. These things will not be consumed and will turn into unsightly trash. Do not burn plastic containers and bags. When you see litter that is not yours, pick it up anyway, it helps to do it. When possible, recycle soda cans, plastic bottles, and waste paper, etc.

Organizations & Government Programs

There are government programs and other organizations that offer information and volunteer projects that you may want to be a part of to do what you can do to help. You may contact these organizations for free information on what they do, statistics, environmental issues, and possible membership.

1.   U.S. Forest Service
   "Keep America Beautiful"
   P.O. Box 96090
   Washington, D.C. 20090-6090

The "KAB" program will plants millions of trees each year in thousands of communities across the country.

2.   National Wildlife Federation
   "Make a Difference"
   Washington, D.C. 20036

This program covers all aspects of environment and conservation. Their information will tell you what you can do to help in your community and area.

3.   Ducks Unlimited
   1 Waterfoul Way
   Memphis TN 38120

DU is dedicated to providing habitat for water birds such as ducks and geese, and other wildlife that lives in or near the water. DU wants to stop over development in certain areas where wildlife is threatened.

4.   The Nature Conservancy
      Suite 800 N. Kent Street
      Arlington VA 22209

 This group is also concerned about natural habitat for wildlife and plant life. It also operates over a thousand nature sanctuaries found across the country.

5.   The Izack Walton League
      1401 Wilson Boulevard, Level B
      Arlington VA 22209

This organization is concerned with air and water quality and the protection of wetlands and public lands.

6.   The Future Fisherman Foundation
      One Berkely Drive
      Spirit Lake IA 51360

This foundation promotes participation and education about fishing and conservation of our natural water resources.

Note: contact addresses may have changed since the writing of this book. Consult internet or other sources to confirm.

Resources List

1.   Reference books used in the writing of this book:

Complete Book of Camping
      Leonard Miracle & Maurice Decker, Harper & Row

Expect the Unexpected, Preparations for Emergency
      American Red Cross

Skills for Taming the Wilds
      Bradford Angier, Stackpole Books

The Book of Survival
      Anthony Greenbank, Harper & Row

Wildwood Wisdom
      Ellsworth Jaeger, The Macmillan Company

2.   Publications by Robert Clemente

A Catalog History of Schrade Knives:
Uncle Henry and Old Timer
      Major Market Publications

Knifery, Complete Handbook of Knife Care and Safety
      Major Market Publications, Kindle Direct Publishing

3.   Papers & Topical Items available upon request:
      Robert Clemente, *clemente@bellsouth.net*

About the Author

Robert Clemente grew up in the Detroit area and soon became an outdoor enthusiast. The areas of camping, hiking, tracking, and survival caught his interests early on, and in high school and college he was instructing in life in the outdoors at boy's and girl's camps and groups in and around Michigan. After college he developed his own audio contracting business that found favor in national and international markets designing and building sound/studio systems.

Robert, holding two bachelor's degrees at the time, moved to Florida with his family to pursue writing and editing projects from ghost writing books, Department of Defense manuals, to recording books for production.

He and his wife and five children moved to the Atlanta area where he finished his teaching certificate to work as a middle school and high school English teacher specializing in reading and writing instruction. He continued work on his Master's degree, Education Specialist's degree, and is now in the final stages of a Doctor of Philosophy in Learning and Literacy.

By his own admission, he credits his early days in the wilds learning not only the wisdom and knowledge of the woods, but more importantly, the skills in resourcefulness and creativity. To those days and times, he is most grateful to those who helped him along the way.

Whoever it was that gave him his first knife, he owes a lifetime of gratitude, but he cannot remember who to thank... he often says, "A knife is a most precious gift, and some cultures believe that when you give someone a knife, you give them part of your soul."

Author's Note about Plagiarism

Please note that although this book is published as of this date, July, 2019 and has been marketed in earlier versions, it is still the intellectual property of Robert Clemente, and his assigns. Under federal law, it cannot be copied or reproduced in any manner, electronic or hard copy, without the express permission of the author. No portion of this book, its concepts, charts, drawings, diagrams, can be used for other publications, online productions, or other media for any purpose, private or commercial without the express, written consent of the author. If a portion of this book is to be used for reference or support, you must obtain permission by the author in writing (electronic, print hard copy, or media), and you must reference the portion in an online citing format. Such permission is for small portions only. Portions of this book may not be used for others' online sites or presentations. If you have any questions pertaining to this policy, please take a moment to contact the author for clarification.

Thank you,

R. Clemente